Shortages of skilled labour have been – and remain – a problem for large parts of Norwegian industry. The position has been eased to some extent by increased recruitment of women for such jobs, including crafts previously dominated by men – as indicated by this scene from Europe's largest plough factory, operated by Kverneland A.S. at Bryne near Stavanger in south-west Norway.

Population (1.1.82):		4.1 million
Main cities:	Oslo	451 789
	Bergen	207 753
	Trondheim	134 983
	Stavanger	90 732
	Kristiansand	60 945
	Drammen	49 533
Life expectancy:		
	Women	79.0 years
	Men	72.3 years

Surface area:		sq.miles
		125 050
Possessions:	Spitzbergen	23 958
	Jan Mayen	144
	Bouvet Island	23
	Peter I Island	96

Continental shelf area: 386 100
(corresponding to 1 million sq.km.)

Coastline, including fjords
and inlets: 13 121 miles

Distribution of area (per cent):

Mountains	62.1
Productive forests	21.3
Islands	6.9
Lakes and rivers	4.8
Agricultural land	3.1
Glaciers	1.4
Cities	0.4

Midnight sun:
Harstad	25 May-17 July
North Cape	12 May-29 July.

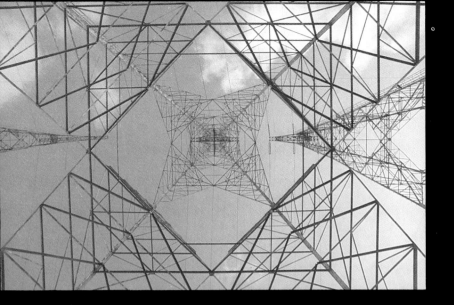

Gross domestic product 1981:
NOK 328 billion (USD 54.8 billion)

GDP per head:	NOK 80 000 (USD 13 330)

Total exports: NOK 155.2 billion
(USD 1 = NOK 6)

Total exports: NOK 156.7 billion
of which
oil and gas: NOK 48.1 billion
commodities: NOK 52.2 billion
freight earnings NOK 31.4 billion

Imports: NOK 130.5 billion

Trade surplus 1981: NOK 26.2 billion

Most important export markets:
UK
West Germany
Sweden
Denmark
USA

Most important sources of imports:
Sweden
West Germany
UK
USA
Denmark

Merchant fleet: 849 ships aggregating
21.4 million tons gross.

North Sea oil production, 1981:
50 million tonnes of oil equivalents, equal to
about 500 000 barrels per day.
Domestic oil consumption: 8 mill. tonnes.

A total of 310 wells had been drilled at
January 1982

Oil and gas fields in production:
Ekofisk area (seven fields)   Murchison
Statfjord   Frigg
Under development:
34/10 Delta-East   North-East Frigg
Heimdal   Valhall A
Odin

Estimated reserves: 4 billion tonnes of oil
equivalents

Total offshore investments up to 1 Jan.
1982: NOK 76 billion (USD 12,7 billion).

new norway 5

By Gunnar Jerman

Layout: Bjørg Omholt

Translated by Rolf Gooderham

THE EXPORT COUNCIL OF NORWAY

GRØNDAHL & SØN A.S

OSLO 1982

An unexpected country

Title pages: Children of the rainbow on the Hardanger-vidda plateau in south-central Norway.

Preceding pages: The Nussfjord fishing village in the Lofoten islands off northern Norway is one of the best preserved timber house environments in the country. Remains of human settlement dating back more than 4 000 years have been found in Lofoten, where a mild climate prevails despite a location as far to the north as Greenland. The Lofoten fishing season is among Norway's most famous and important coastal fisheries.

Above: Folk dance groups for both children and adults – called «leikarringer» – flourish in Norway.

Above right: Modern industrial firms have grown up throughout the country.

NORWAY DIFFERS in many ways from the image most foreigners hold of the country. Old industries such as fishing, trapping, catching and shipping, snow-covered mountains and deep fjords characterise this misconception. Today's reality is otherwise, and a variety of modern manufacturing activities form the economic backbone of Norway as in other industrialised countries.

One of Norway's leading newspapers recently carried out a survey through its many foreign correspondents to establish just how much foreigners really know about Norway.

Their findings revealed that knowledge about the country is not particularly widespread in the rest of the world. Some of those polled thought the Norwegian population must lie between 40 and 100 million people, and that they possibly speak French. A larger group was convinced that the Polar bear is a daily sight, if not in the streets then at least outside the towns in northern Norway.

Nor were those asked in doubt that the Norwegian climate is uncomfortably cold, but added that the country could nevertheless be well worth a visit because of the beautiful fjords, mountains and girls with long fair hair.

Outside Europe, people asked to describe Norway's location placed it right up in the corner of the map – not so far from the end of the world.

The four million Norwegians will have to concede that they live near the world's end, with the Atlantic Ocean and Norwegian Sea as close – but thanks to the Gulf Stream not particularly chill – neighbours. The many fjords that carve their way into the land between majestic mountains and the waterfalls which plunge down the precipitous mountainsides give Norwegian

Below: The «Markeds Gade» pedestrian precinct in Kristiansand, the main city of southern Norway.

Top right: White-painted wooden houses are a prominent element in south Norwegian architecture, as here at Rasvaagen on Hidra island outside Flekkefjord.

Bottom right: The Henrikke open-air restaurant outside the National Theatre in Oslo provides an attractive refuge in the light summer evenings.

nature its special character and beauty. Summers can often be warm and sun-filled, even though most of the population find them too short for their taste.

Norwegian is the language spoken, of course, and it lies so close to Swedish and Danish that all Scandinavians can understand each other without much difficulty. Living conditions in the Nordic countries are much the same in many respects, in fact. The Polar bear is not found in any of them, only on the islands far to the north on the edge of the Arctic Ocean.

People in Norway must also admit that not many of their number are well-known to the world at large. A long time has passed since a

Nobel Prize was last awarded to a Norwegian, for instance, and decades since Thor Heyerdahl sailed his *Kon Tiki* and *Ra* vessels on their adventurous voyages across the oceans.

Naturally enough, Norwegians continue to win gold medals in world championship events for national sports like skiing and ice skating, but it is a generation since the figure skating queen Sonia Henie and the ski-jumper Birger Ruud caught the imagination of an international public – and two generations since Roald Amundsen planted the very first flag at the South Pole and another great Polar explorer, Fridtjof Nansen, set off for the North Pole on skis.

Any country is in continual change, and living conditions can alter quickly. A small country is also subject to influence from abroad. This applies equally to Norway, where movements in the international economy can strongly affect many areas in the life of the community. Norwegians, too, have been forced to recognise – with some surprise after decades of unbroken economic growth – that progress and prosperity are not a matter of course but call for properly directed effort and the right use of resources.

If social and economic conditions alter, however, some factors never change. In Norway's case, this applies first and foremost to the natural environment together with a location on the European fringe. Climate, distance and ceaseless struggle with the forces of Nature are part of life's pattern.

Geography has produced an uneven population distribution, with long distances separating people in many parts of the country. Most of the towns have developed along the coast as centres for trade and communication. They are small by international standards, but have nevertheless not managed entirely to avoid the same urban problems we see in other countries.

Half of Norway's inhabitants live in the southeastern region known as *Østlandet,* with a particularly heavy concentration in the districts round Oslo, the capital, and the Oslo Fjord.

The Norwegian continental shelf is three times

Below: Forests cover almost a quarter of Norway. The wood processing industry is an important factor in the national economy, and timber floating from felling sites to the mills formerly played a crucial role in this sector. Although the bulk of the wood is transported by road today, timber floaters are still at work in many places.

Right: The land of fjords and mountains can also boast broad farmland districts, as on the eastern shores of Lake Mjøsa, Norway's largest stretch of inland water. This is the most important grain-growing region in the country, with big farms and field succeeding field as far as the eye can see.

as large as the country's total land area. This shelf is the source of Norway's offshore oil and gas wealth. By the early 1980's, the Norwegians were already Europe's first net oil exporters.

Several substantial oil and gas finds are either in production or under development, while exploration along the coast continues to provide fresh discoveries. At the same time, it has become clear that Norway will remain dependent on its traditional industrial and commercial activities in the future to maintain the country's economic strength and preserve the benefits that have been created.

Norway's natural resources in many ways place this northern nation in a unique position. In addition to oil and gas, the country can boast large supplies of hydro-electric power from its mountain rivers and coal from the Svalbard islands in the remote north.

Opportunities for leading a free and open life are also an important resource, and Norway has special advantages in this respect. With only four million people in Europe's fifth largest country by land area, such opportunities are more than sufficient.

This book seeks to paint a picture of a many-sided nation that extends across 13 degrees of latitude from Lindesnes in the south to the North Cape – equal to the distance from Norway's southern tip to central Italy. This span is itself an indication of why the country offers such varied living conditions and possibilities.

Summer – days with no nights

The seasons have a special significance in Norway. There are pronounced differences between them and they do not shift imperceptibly from one to the other as in countries further south.

When summer finally comes, the weather can be just as warm as in southern Europe. Even northern Norway can be among the warmest European regions for weeks on end.

But the Norwegians live with highly changeable climate, and there is a lot of truth in the old saying that «no-one knows how the day will turn out until the sun goes down». Pouring rain or fog's clammy hand can swiftly replace the glint of sun on the mountains, particularly in northern and western Norway.

Nobody can be certain when Nature will give of its bounty and how long the pleasure will last. So Norwegians take full advantage of the opportunity when the chance occurs, and pour out to cabins, boats, islands, lakes, mountains and forests.

Summer in Norway is boating, Midsummer's Night bonfires along the fjords, campers and angling, the great communal holiday that everybody looks forward to. This is the season when Norway shrugs off its winter skin – the animals to summer colours, the girls to light dresses.

Day ceases to give way to dark for a time in the north, and even in southern parts of the country the nights are short and light.

Above: Summer in Portør, where eastern and southern Norway meet and merge.

Right: Nature itself creates the most beautiful works of art.

Autumn –
nature clad in yellows and reds

The autumn is Norway's loveliest season, when Nature adorns itself with the most delightful colours in shades of yellow and red. These autumn tints stand out sharply against the mountains which have already donned their winter garb.

Autumn nights in Norway mean myriads of stars speckling the high dark vault of the August heavens as cool winds add a chill touch to the air. This is the time of the first night frosts, rime on brown straw and grassy slopes, and the first thin ice on ponds and pools. Phosphorescence glows along boat gunwales on mirror-calm evenings when the crab fishing among the islands and rocks is at its best.

Inland, berries carpet the ground in forest and bog – yellow cloudberries, Norway's favourite dessert, red cranberries and blue bilberries. Mushrooms abound, too, at this time of harvest.

Autumn is also the hunting season, for reindeer and grouse in mountains and elk or woodland birds in the forest.

The new school year starts, and the Storting – Norway's Parliament – reassembles for a further session at the beginning of October. By then, winter is just around the corner.

Above: September is the hunting season.

Right: The Rondane mountains of central Norway in autumn finery.

Wintersport as a lifestyle

The long Norwegian winter has its own distinctive character. It starts out dark and damp, and then becomes white, dry and cold. Later on, the snowy landscape gets lighter before the sun begins to get a grip during March, relieving the trees of their heavy snow burdens and bathing the highland slopes in light towards Easter.

Winter in Norway is the indoor season, white Christmasses and Easter sunshine with snow crystals sparkling like diamonds. Hard storms rage, frost hangs like smoke over open lakes and ski tracks wind through the countryside.

This is also the season for Norway's national sports, dear to the heart of Norwegians. The top skiers and ice skaters enjoy high status and are treated like the world's leading sporting stars.

But Norwegians are not simply passive spectators of the ski-racer's fight against clock and competitor. A large number of cross-country skiing contests are arranged every weekend – the biggest with up to 10 000 participants.

Skiing is part of a Norwegian's lifestyle. Many decades of winter trips in forest and field lie between the first uncertain steps in child-size ski boots and the pensioner's more cautious outings across frozen lakes and along easy forest or mountain tracks.

All the towns in Norway are surrounded by networks of long-distance skiing tracks, many of them floodlit for evening use.

Above: In free flight high over Oslo.

Right: Winter landscape from Rondane in central Norway.

Spring – waking up again

Excitement characterises spring in Norway, as the young and the fresh make their debut. This is the season of preparation – cleaning boats that will soon be back in the water, putting summer cabins into order, sowing for farmer and gardener and the younger generation taking examinations that are a preparation for life itself.

Spring means longer days and shorter nights, melting snow, streams that turn into rivers and small rapids that become cascading waterfalls. Beech trees spring into leaf more or less overnight, while crocuses make their appearance along with blue and white anemones and pussy willows.

May 17 is Constitution Day, when high school graduates start the «russ» celebrations that are intended to be a last fling before entering the serious world of university studies.

Animals end their winter hibernation, while flocks of swallows and other migrant birds come north once again. Fruit trees blossom, bicycles are brought out from winter store and the Bergen International Festival greets spring with an explosion of music, art and drama.

The season also works its magic on the human spirit. People melt with the snow they have lived through – put on thin clothes too soon, exploit every stray beam of spring sunshine, and fall in love. They experience the same spring thaw that nature does.

Above: The newly-qualified student generation is called «russ» and adds a colourful element to the spring with its red clothes.

Right: Winter does not relax its grip on everything equally easily, even on Constitution Day itself. Commemorating the adoption of Norway's present constitution in 1814, May 17 is celebrated by children's processions all over the country – including Finse, the highest point on the railway line linking Oslo and Bergen across the central Norwegian highlands.

Rainy days bring good fortune

WATER PERMEATES the Norwegian landscape and gives it life, flowing from the mountain fastnesses that cover two-thirds of the country and from close to 200 000 small lakes. On their way to the sea through the forest regions of eastern Norway and down precipitous mountainsides in the west, the rivers make their contribution to the special character of the countryside.

«It's an ill wind that blows nobody any good,» the proverb says, and that also applies to the wet Atlantic winds which blow in over Norway from the west, bringing rain and snow to the considerable inconvenience and annoyance of the inhabitants. Through the harnessing of hydro-electric power, however, these masses of humid air created the basis for the country's power-intensive industries.

Norway is rich in energy resources. A substantial proportion of its power consumption is provided by electricity. Large oil and gas reserves exist on the continental shelf and the coal measures on Svalbard are thought to contain 200-300 million tonnes of this fuel.

Hydro-power development can cause unsightly scars in nature and therefore meets strong opposition from environmentalists. But hydro-electricity has considerable environmental advantages, too, since it does not cause any atmospheric pollution. This energy source is also self-renewing as long as moist air continues to flow constantly in over Norway.

At the moment, only about half of Norway's total water power resources have been harnessed. Many rivers are protected from development for environmental reasons, which in turn set a limit to continued expansion in hydro-power generating capacity.

Preceding page: The Jotunheimen mountain range in central Norway can boast a majestic beauty and wild grandeur. Pictured here is the Gjende lake in the heart of Jotunheimen – which incidentally means «land of giants». The Beseggen ridge divides Gjende from the Bessvann lake, lying some 400 metres higher. It was here that Henrik Ibsen placed Peer Gynt's wild ride on the buck, and plunge into the water.

Above: Salmon leap in Norway's foaming waterfalls.

Right: Aluminium is processed power. From Karmøy Fabrikker near Haugesund on the west coast.

Development of hydro-electric power in Norway began almost exactly a century ago. But the great bulk of the generating capacity has been installed since 1945.

The whole country is today covered by a single national supply grid, which connects in turn with the Swedish and Danish power systems. Norway exports power in years with plenty of precipitation, while in very dry periods it buys electricity from thermal power stations fueled by coal or oil in Sweden and Denmark.

Norwegian electro-technical industry has developed in line with the country's electrification, and most of the equipment for power stations and transmission lines comes from Norwegian suppliers. Substantial expertise has been built up, not least in the field of power transmission technology.

Norwegian firms have in recent years been responsible for planning, building and delivering a number of hydro-power projects world-wide, both in the developing countries and in Western industrialised nations.

One of the largest contracts obtained in this field covers the laying of submarine transmission cables in Canada, an assignment that builds on experience and know-how gained from work with similar cables linking Norway and Denmark.

Left: Production of power station equipment at NEBB in Oslo.

Below: New hydro-power plants call for equipment with very large dimensions. Transport of such units on construction access roads in the mountains or through towns and villages often creates problems. A turbine housing supplied by Kværner Brug of Oslo for the Aurland power station is seen here being moved through the Aurlandsvangen valley near the head of Norway's longest fjord, the Sogne Fjord on the west coast.

Below: Most new power stations are blasted into the mountain. Norwegian blasting techniques have won international recognition. This technology has long traditions in a country where road and rail tunnels, dams and extensive preparation of construction sites are essential.

The generator hall for the Aurland II station has impressive dimensions, measuring 100 metres in length and 30 metres from floor to ceiling. Inlet pipes for the turbines are under installation here.

Right: Helicopters are often the only way of delivering equipment to power plant developments in the impassable Norwegian mountains. Ready-mixed concrete is here being flown up to a dam construction site by the Bondhusbreen, an arm of the great Folgefonna glacier. Tunnels have been blasted alongside the 170 metre-thick ice layer and the concrete is landed at the eagle's nest that provides accommodation and an installation site, perched on the cliff face a few metres from the glacier.

Norway accounts for a fifth of Europe's aluminium output with an annual production capacity of 700 000 tonnes, and ranks as the largest European exporter of this important light metal. Årdal og Sunndal Verk (ÅSV), Elkem and Norsk Hydro are the largest producers.

Secure access to plenty of hydro-electric power makes this production possible. With three smelters in Høyanger, Årdal and Sunndal on the west coast, ÅSV accounts for almost exactly half the Norwegian output and is one of the country's largest electricity consumers – reflecting the fact that it takes 15 000 kWh to produce one tonne of aluminium.

Pictured here is Lista, one of Elkem's two aluminium plants.

Below: High power consumption and environmental considerations have necessitated a comprehensive modernisation of some plants, including the installation of fume-free and energy-saving pots. Høyanger Verk at the head of the Sogne Fjord has recently completed a thorough-going rationalisation.

Bottom and right; Norsk Hydro is boosting its production capacity at Karmøy Fabrikker on the west coast by 47 000 tonnes of aluminium through the construction of two new electrolysis halls. Half of the plant's future annual output of 160 000 tonnes will be further processed on Karmøy.

Magnesium is one of the commonest elements found in nature. Every tonne of seawater, for instance, contains 1.3 kg. of this light metal. But magnesium refining calls for substantial amounts of energy.

Norsk Hydro began magnesium production in the early 1950's at Herøya on the Oslo Fjord, and ranks today as the western world's largest manufacturer of the metal – which is a quarter of the weight of steel and a third lighter than aluminium.

As the lightest of all metals used for fabrication, it has a broad range of applications in alloy form. The car industry, where weight has become an increasingly important factor, accounts for most of the consumption.

Production techniques for magnesium have hitherto been complex, but many years of research at Hydro resulted in the development of a new processing method. A plant employing this technology – which provides substantial economic and environmental advantages – recently began operation.

Raw materials for magnesium production are available in large quantities and include seawater, dolomite from northern Norway and magnesium chloride from Germany. After an initial treatment, the calcinated dolomite is mixed with seawater in large outdoor settling tanks and magnesium oxide extracted as a precipitate.

Liquid primary magnesium is then produced in electrolytic cells before being cast into ingots and sold to industry for use in a number of different products.

Two major organisations – Fesil and Elkem – make Norway the world's leading exporter of ferro-alloys.

Elkem is the world's leading producer of ferro-alloys and has holdings in three US plants and an Icelandic plant, in addition to six smelters in Norway.

Through its engineering division, the company is also the chief international supplier of smelter technology to the ferro-alloy industry.

The picture below is from Salten Verk, which lies north of the Arctic Circle and ranks as Europe's largest and most modern ferro-alloy plant with an annual capacity of 85 000 tonnes.

Fesil is the sales organisation for four other Norwegian ferro-alloy producers.

Glomfjord Fabrikker, one of Norsk Hydro's many subsidiaries, also lies above the Arctic Circle close to the Svartisen glacier. In these magnificent surroundings, Hydro produces the bulk of the fertiliser used within Norway.

Hydro's fertiliser production marked the beginning of serious exploitation of Norwegian water power potential when it started in 1905 – the same year that Norway gained its independence. At that time, Norway was a developing country, one of the poorest in Europe.

Two new urban communities, Rjukan and Notodden, were established near the power sources which made fertiliser production possible. This product area remains important for Hydro even today, with production in a number of countries outside Norway.

But the company's output also embraces aluminium, magnesium, petrochemical products, and a range of finished products. The biggest growth area for Hydro in recent years has been its steadily expanding involvement in oil and gas exploration, production and processing.

The Norwegian mining industry has long traditions. Iron ore was being produced as far back as the early Iron Age, and the basis was laid for a modern mining industry 350 years ago with the copper mines at Røros in central Norway and silver production at Kongsberg in the south-east.

These historic mines are now closed down, but small mining communities have grown up in a number of other places around the country.

Most Norwegian ores have been located accidentally, by hunters, anglers and reindeer herders. The same is true of the country's largest copper mine at Sulitjelma in northern Norway (pictured on this page). Like the other Norwegian mines, ore reserves here are small by international standards.

A century will soon have passed since operations began at Sulitjelma, which has Norway's only smelter for copper. A few thousand people live in this little community in the heart of the mountains close to the border with Sweden and just above the Arctic Circle a couple of hours drive from Bodø. The ore is mined 500 metres below ground.

The mines revert to the Norwegian state in 1983, and Elkem – the company responsible for operating them today – has announced that it does not want to continue these operations. A uncertain future accordingly faces the mining community under the Pole Star, because like so many other small Norwegian towns it has been built up entirely around a single company.

38

Reindeer are often associated with Norway's only significant ethnic minority, the Lapps, who live in the northernmost part of the country. Only a few of the 20 000 or so Norwegian Lapps make a living from reindeer herding today, however. In addition, Europe's largest herds of wild reindeer are found in the Norwegian mountains further south.

Thousands of these animals graze on the Hardangervidda plateau *(below)*. Their numbers declined for a time, but have now recovered to the point where the reindeer herds are again as large as the region can support. They provide a popular and much-loved sight for visitors to the mountains, and naturally for hunters during the autumn hunting season.

Wildlife in the wilderness

ANIMAL LIFE in Norway is the result of a conflict between nature and civilisation. Where people built and hunted, other creatures had to retreat. But the distribution of various animal species was also affected by climatic changes. Milder weather conditions caused the natural habitat of Arctic fauna to retreat, while animals from more temperate regions moved into these areas and pushed out the original species.

Norway extends across 13 degrees of latitude from south to north. Eastern regions characterised by warm summers and cold, snowy winters contrast with the mild west coast climate where temperatures remain relatively constant all year round. These conditions set their stamp on animal life.

The differences in climate have also contributed to a virtual division of the country between the various big game animals. As a result, the elk – King of the Forest – lords it over the forest lands of the east, deer dominate western districts and reindeer occupy the highlands.

Life in the sea has always been of the greatest economic significance in Norway. From earliest times, catching of sea creatures such as seals and whales played a major role in the food supply. Fishing was nevertheless the commonest source of provisions for Norwegians, and fish also provided the first significant trading commodity for large groups of the population.

Not only people but also animals acquired much of their food from the sea, forging close links between creatures on land and in the water. This applies particularly to Norwegian birds – and the thousands of islands and rich food resources along the coast offer particularly favourable living conditions for seabirds.

Some feathered species live scattered, but the most prominent feature of animal life in Norway's coastlands are the vast cliffside nesting colonies, where hundreds of thousands of birds can often be found. They nest so close together in these «communities» that the birds nearly touch and at the height of the breeding season it is impossible to climb the cliffs without stepping on eggs.

Foreigners think of Arctic animals such as reindeer, Polar bears, seals and walruses as being typically Norwegian. These species have adapted to the climatic conditions in which they live and exploit their natural surroundings to the full. Not only are they covered in thick fur as a protection against extreme cold, but these animals also have to be capable of living for much of the year on little food.

The next few pages will take a closer look at some of Norway's native land animals.

Below: A new-born roe deer fawn lies hidden quite motionlessly for several days in the blueberry ling. Being left alone as much as possible gives the fawn its best chance of survival and of avoiding disturbances. The mother gives it milk two to three times a day and after a little while the young creature is strong enough to follow its parent into the forest.

Following pages: Encountering baby Tengmalm's owls like these four appealing characters ranks among the greatest delights of the June woodlands. There is a four-day age difference between this group, which accounts for the variations in size. The parents feed the young for several weeks after birth, usually at dusk.

A poll conducted by the Norwegian Broadcasting Corporation some years ago resulted in the election of the regal elk as Norway's national animal. This King of the Forest is found in most woodland regions and its numbers are greater than ever before.

The elk is well-adapted to Norwegian nature and copes well with deep snow and cold. If food runs short, it will move closer to the towns and villages and sometimes finds its way right into the heart of the big cities.

Summer is the best time for the elk, with good grazing conditions and plenty of water. In this season, it often gravitates to lakes or ponds.

Right: An elk cow with two calves rests in a small glade in the spruce forest. When young elk calves are twins, they normally lie close enough for body contact.

Below: Bears, wolves, wolverines and lynx are all regarded as threatened species in Norway, even if the number of bears and lynx have again begun to increase.

Like many other predators, the lynx is nocturnal and remains by and large quiescent during the day. This picture is the first taken of a wild adult lynx in Norway.

Top right: In late autumn, the red squirrel acquires its long-haired winter coat with tall tufts of hair on the ears. Once dressed for the cold weather, it can tolerate extremely low temperatures. But the squirrel needs a snug shelter at night since, unlike most other Norwegian mammals, it lies down to a regular night's sleep throughout the year.

Bottom right: The red fox is a night hunter. Much of the daytime is devoted to sleep and rest – but this does not mean that it always goes to bed with the dawn. In the winter it can be active day and night to keep hunger at bay.

Left: You have to be out of bed early to catch a capercaillie performing its mating ritual. This large forest bird begins its distinctive calls and ecstatic «dance» in the service of reproduction before sunrise. But those fortunate enough to be able to observe the mating game deep in the woods are participating in one of the great spring ceremonies of the Norwegian forests.

Below: On watch in a kittiwake colony in northern Norway.

Bottom left: The odd and colourful horned grebe nesting on the north Norwegian coast.

Bottom right: The black-throated diver is a great catcher of fish, and consumes a variety of species. Its legs are positioned so far back that they are virtually useless on land – so this bird nests on the edge of the shore and can slip easily into the water when it senses danger.

The Arctic environment harbours few animal species. The Polar bear is the largest land creature to live in these regions. It can reach a length of three metres and weigh 500-600 kg.

Those who think that Polar bears dwell in and around Norwegian towns are mistaken. The only specimens of this animal in mainland Norway are stuffed and stand outside souvenir shops. Its home is the islands of the Arctic Ocean and it can commonly be found in the Svalbard archipelago. Many tales are told about the Polar bear's curiosity, and the beast is jokingly said to wander around Svalbard secure in the knowledge of its status as a protected species.

Despite its size, the Polar bear moves with feline elegance and is quick on its paws when hunting for seal or fish in the ice-fringed seas. Major research programmes are being conducted with the aim of discovering more about the animal's lifestyle. Males and females associate only during the breeding season. Once the cubs are born, they follow the mother for two years.

A total of 470 fish farms are registered in Norway, and specialise mostly in the raising of Atlantic salmon *(salmo salar)* and rainbow trout *(salmo irideus)*. Experimental work is also being done on the farming of lobster and other sea fish varieties, and cultivation of mussels and oysters will be greatly expanded over the next few years.

Some of the farms are substantial, like the attractive facility operated by Ole Torrissen & Sønner at Halsa in Nordland county. Situated just north of the Arctic Circle, this installation is well protected by the skerries fringing the coast.

The clear, clean waters all along the Norwegian coast are ideal for fish farming and the Gulf Stream ensures favourable temperatures and rapid growth both summer and winter.

Fish move to the farm

FISH WAS ONE of Norway's first export commodities and has played a crucial role in the economy of the coastal population ever since the first settlement 7 000 years ago.

This industry remains highly important for the community, particularly in northern Norway. Fishing accounts for more than 30 per cent of all jobs in 34 of the country's 454 municipalities, and fish-related activities are frequently the only source of employment – especially in the far northern country of Finnmark.

As a result, the fishing industry plays a major part in efforts to conserve the settlement pattern along the north Norwegian coast.

Although the number of fishermen has declined and only about 17 000 people are solely employed in fishing today, activities linked with the fisheries provide jobs for 80 000 workers in boatbuilding, production of fishing gear, transport and nearly 700 processing plants. Another 13 000 people have fishing as a subsidiary occupation, mostly in combination with farming.

The total catch has stayed at more than two million tonnes a year for several decades. Capelin, a small fish of the salmon family, accounts for more than half of this quantity, but the cod fishery is nevertheless the most important in economic terms and represents roughly two-thirds of the first-hand catch value.

Fish farming or acquaculture is the fastest-growing sector of the fishing industry. Production of Atlantic salmon and rainbow trout from these fjord farms will reach 15 000 tonnes in 1982, and should be up to 25 000 tonnes by the mid-1980's – when salmon and trout will long have become the most important commercial fish species after cod.

Above: Harvesting work down on the fish farm.

Top right: Seen here testing cod appetites, Norwegian research workers are currently seeking ways of feeding cod fry in hatcheries. If this can be accomplished in the manner already achieved with trout and salmon, it will be possible to transplant the cultivated fry to build up local cod stocks.

Researchers claim that cod are easy to control and grow rapidly. A single fish can put on a kilogram within a few months when fed with the equivalent of two kg. of capelin. Cases have been reported of a 60-gram cod reaching four kg. within nine months.

Bottom right: Cultivated fish are fed on a special diet where capelin and fish meal are the main ingredients. The Torrislaks company has built this plant to ensure that the fish get the right diet.

It is a long step from the primitive fishing vessels of earlier times to today's modern ships. Thanks to their effective equipment and advanced fishing techniques, the catch capacity of the latter has become too great – resulting in over-exploitation of the sea's resources.

For this reason, a considerable proportion of the sea-going fishing fleet is now subject to highly restrictive quotas, and other measures are being implemented in a bid to reduce the number of vessels.

Problems associated with a diminished raw material base affect all fishing nations, and steps to re-build fish stocks have accordingly been launched at both national and international levels. These efforts are beginning to produce results and the future looks brighter. The new law of the sea rules concerning the creation of 200-mile economic zones, in particular, give Norway the opportunity to exploit its fish resources in a better way than before.

The primitive fishing methods of yesterday have been replaced by modern techniques and equipment which give the fish little chance of evading capture. Computerised tracking systems are employed to locate the shoals and fishing gear is shaped and dimensioned for maximum efficiency – marking a fundamental contrast to the far-off days when Norwegian fishermen initiated the activity that was to grow into the country's first export industry.

Today's advanced technology for harvesting the seas has helped to over-tax available fish resources, making it necessary to introduce stringent catch restrictions aimed at preventing the disappearance of some species and preserving stocks for the future.

Comprehensive production of equipment and gear for fishing and fish processing has been built up over generations in Norway. Several hundred firms founded to serve the fishing fleet are spread all along the country's lengthy coast. Neither boat-builders nor suppliers of all other types of gear remain restricted to the domestic market, however, but have found fresh outlets for their skills and experience throughout the world. Norwegian fishing equipment and fish processing plant find ready buyers in Latin America, Canada, Alaska, the Far East and Africa, as well as in Europe.

Even with every kind of modern and effective technique to hand, experience and know-how remain the decisive factors for success in this ancient industry. The same applies to the production of fishing gear like today's huge seine nets, where Norway has naturally acquired a wealth of experience. This picture shows net-making at A/S Fiskernes Redskaps-fabrikk in Finnsnes on the north Norwegian coast.

60

A chain of 700 plants along the coast processes the raw materials harvested from the sea. The largest number of jobs is provided by the frozen fish sector, where marketing is handled by large combines. Frionor ranks as the biggest of these, and sells products from about 120 freezing plants.

Various forms of dried or salted fish are produced by a network of processing companies. The fish canning factories have recently combined in the Norway Food company, while the fish meal producers sell their output through the Nordsildmel organisation.

Above: Hamnøy in the Lofoten islands above the Arctic Circle is ringed by majestic mountains. As with so many other settlements in these islands, fishing provides the most important economic activity.

Right: Øksfjord lies in Finnmark, the largest county in Norway but with the fewest inhabitants.

Far right: Climatic conditions in northern Norway are ideal for drying fish in the open, where they can be exposed to the cold dry wind. One kilogram of the final dried product corresponds to five kg. of fresh fish.

62

When 4 000 fishermen have returned home after the hectic weeks of the winter Lofoten fishery, calm descends on the hundreds of «rorbu» cabins that gave the men a temporary home in the fishing villages along the Vestfjord coast and in Vesterålen.

But this peace is soon broken again when visitors of all ages move into the red-painted cabins in search of the holiday with a difference. Like the professional fishermen, they catch both cod and saithe – partly for food and partly for the sport.

Increasingly popular, a rorbu holiday offers a quiet and carefree break away from stress and exhaust fumes and guides and tourist hordes. It gives a chance, too, of experiencing a summer morning like this in Toppsundet near Harstad, secure in the knowledge that the saithe and cod are biting well.

Getting away from it all

NORWEGIANS POSSESS enough of the great outdoors to escape from their neighbours if they want. The vast majority of people in Norway are admittedly city-dwellers, as in most other countries. But as soon as the occasion offers itself, the Norwegians shake the dust of the town from their feet and set off for the nearest uninhabited spot where they can have nature to themselves.

One way of escaping into the country, for instance, is to penetrate far into the mountains on foot during summertime, hiking from cabin to cabin in mist and fog or the most glittering sunshine – and always in the freshest of air.

The mountains also beckon in the winter, with their long stick-marked ski tracks that wind over the open uplands between the tourist cabins.

Outdoor life can involve messing about in boats along the coast, too. The Norwegians have boats in the blood, which is hardly surprising given the manifold opportunities for sailing or motor cruising offered by the long coast with its many fjords and countless offshore islands and islets. Norway has a total of 400 000 registered pleasure craft – one for every third family – ranging from boats for a quick evening trip to fish for cod or mackerel to family-sized cruisers.

This is a country for the sophisticated tourist, who has long since experienced the world's great cities or crowded beach life in more southerly climes. Norway offers the alternative holiday that more and more people seem to need as an escape from mass tourism or the more conventional pleasures of sun, people and night life. A new and different experience can be found here in the form of peace, calm and the enjoyment of nature off the beaten industrialised track.

The Norwegian Royal Family is well-known for its sporting interests and takes an active part in competitive sport. Although he will soon be 80 years old, HM King Olav V is still a keen regatta sailor, and the Crown Prince and Princess share this involvement while ensuring that their two children keep up the family traditions.

But the most energetic among Norway's Royals remains Crown Princess Sonja. She is a trained ski instructress, took part earlier in slalom competitions, participates in the annual Holmenkollen March cross-country ski race outside Oslo and is a keen mountain hiker – seen resting here on Holegga in Sunnmøre, west Norway.

Below: West of the Jotunheimen mountains and north of the Sogne Fjord in western Norway lies Breheimen with Jostedalsbreen – Europe's largest mainland glacier – at its heart. Jostedalsbreen covers 800 sq.km. when all its tongues are included. Breheimen's great scenic beauty makes the region a popular tourist area.

Here the traveller has reached Flatbreskaret and can look out across the Fjærlands Fjord, an arm of the Sogne Fjord.

Right: Climbers from many countries make pilgrimages to the Norwegian mountains. These highlands were more peaceful a century ago when the first pioneers mastered peaks like Store Skagastølstind, Norway's third highest pinnacle. The first man to the summit was the British climber William Cecil Slingsby. Red-clad figures ascend the Slingsby Route through the mist of a July morning. Experienced mountaineers no longer regard this peak as particularly demanding, but ordinary tourists must still remain content with admiring it from a distance.

Below: Finse on the Bergen-Oslo railway is the starting point for some of the finest treks that the Norwegian highlands have to offer. Holiday-makers at Easter head south of the rail tracks towards the sun across the unique Hardangervidda plateau, while to the north lie the magnificent mountain regions around the Hallingskarvet. This dog team is on its way from Finse to Raggsteindalen.

Right: Oslo is justly called the Skiing Capital. On Sundays when skiing conditions are good, a large propor-

tion of the 800 000 people who live in and around this city are to be found out on the many ski trails.

The forested slopes and small lakes known as the Oslomarka make up three-quarters of the city area, and are closed to motor traffic as well as house construction. Snow covers the «marka» throughout the winter and a network of tracks provide plenty of opportunities for experienced skiers and beginners alike. The skiers pictured here are crossing the Krokskogen district on the western edge of the Oslomarka.

Above: Norway's forests and mountains are the land of trolls and huldra nymphs. Tales about trolls and supernatural beings abound, as witnessed by place names such as Trollheimen, Trollfjorden, Trollelven, Trolldalen, Troldhaugen and Trollbukta. The gazetteer of one Norwegian atlas lists 120 names beginning with «troll», including eight Trolldaler (Troll Valley) and eight Trollvann (Troll Lake). Belief in the beautiful but dangerous mountain nymphs with their cow tails has been commemorated, too, in names such as Hulderkyrkk, Hulderheimen and Huldrestølen. Evidence of genuine trolls carved from the Norwegian mountains is given by this picture from Børgefjell national park on the Helgeland cost in the north.

Right: Evening on Lake Femunden in eastern Norway.

72

Summer days by the fjords or a first foray for river trout can provide the spark for nascent anglers. The gear might be home-made and simple, but these childhood experiences yield the know-how about fish movements and lifestyle that the more sophisticated adult angler needs when tackling bigger prey.

Norway's 200 000 lakes, spread across forest and fell, together with thousands of rivers and streams, offer rich opportunities for varied and exciting fishing expeditions by the 190 000 registered Norwegian anglers. On pay-

ment of a small fee, which is mainly used to fund improved fishing facilities, anyone can fish more or less anywhere apart from most of the 200 registered salmon rivers. The latter are reserved for those who can pay the large sums demanded by the landowners for rod rights.

Many of the salmon fishermen are foreigners who return to the same river year after year. The Tana River in Finnmark far to the north occupies a class of its own as Norway's very best salmon river, where 50 000 kg. salmon are caught in the course of a summer.

When the spring sun at long last casts its warming rays over Oslo, the thousands who have enjoyed the Oslo-marka throughout the winter turn their faces to the fjord that runs south from the city for 100 km until it meets the sea at Færder lighthouse.

The Oslo Fjord is said to be home to no less than 130 000 pleasure boats of all sizes and prices, ranging from luxury craft with costly fittings to rowing boats where a couple of oars are the only accessories. But large outlays are by no means necessary in order to enjoy the

pleasures of the fjord, since numerous islands, rocks, bays and sounds provide plenty of shelter for the cheapest craft.

Thousands of summer cabins also line the Oslo Fjord, which ranks as the country's most popular holiday area. Large numbers of people use the numerous camping sites, too, while many more spend their days and evenings on the water as armadas of pleasure craft moor during the summer nights in the idyllic bays. The largest motor cruisers lie side by side with the characteristically

Norwegian snekke – pointed fore and aft – that most family budgets can accommodate.

Even if the equipment on board differs, however, the mussels grilled on the rocks, the cod fished from the water or the prawns bought from fishermen and peeled on deck are the same for everyone.

Left: The annual Færder regatta from Oslo to the lighthouse and back attracts close to a thousand participants.

Below: Training for a future Færder race.

More than half of the 849 vessels in the Norwegian merchant fleet are purpose-built to carry specific products. This kind of specialisation plays a crucial part in allowing a high-cost country like Norway to continue operating one of the world's largest fleets.

During the past 20 years, Norwegian shipping companies have built up a leading international role in the transport of cars by sea. These include Høegh-Ugland Auto Liners A/S, which operates a fleet of specialised carriers for cars, buses, tractors and other vehicles. Pictured here is the company's Europa terminal in Amsterdam.

Cars - crude - chemicals - cruises

SHIPPING IS NORWAY'S most international industry, and the Norwegian merchant fleet ranks as the sixth largest in the world. A glance at the map shows why the sea has always been important for the Norwegian community and how it became the natural highway for the whole country. High mountains and steep-sided ridges hamper land transport, but the coast stays ice-free all year round.

An indication of today's ship sizes is given by the fact that Norway's total annual oil consumption corresponds to no more than 20 cargoes on a fully-laden supertanker. The average vessel has quadrupled in size compared with those of 20 years ago. At the same time, however, the number of ships in the fleet has declined.

Approximately 200 privately-owned Norwegian shipping companies compete for cargoes on the international market. Many of these firms have pioneered the introduction of innovatory vessel types in a bid to boost their chances in the battle for business. Most of Norway's ships never visit a home port, but carry commodities between third countries.

A large part of the Norwegian fleet has been built for the transport of energy in one form or another. Crude oil tankers averaging 170 000 tonnes deadweight in size thus account for more than 50 per cent of the tonnage.

When the hunt for oil and gas at sea began to gather momentum, Norwegian shipowners were in a good position to apply their accumulated maritime expertise and experience to this new field. Today, such companies are actively involved in offshore exploration and development world-wide, including the operation of 30 mobile rigs – 10 per cent of the world fleet.

Specialised carriers for gas and chemicals are relative newcomers to the world shipping industry. Operating such vessels is a complex and expensive business. While most gas or chemical tankers are small in relation to oil tankers and bulk carriers, this is not always the case.

The *Høegh Gandris,* pictured below in the Suez Canal, can carry up to 125 900 cu.m. of liquified gas – equivalent to 67 000 tonnes of oil in energy terms. The ship has been built in accordance with the well-known spherical tank design developed by Norwegian shipbuilder Moss Rosenberg Verft, which has become the world's leading type of large gas carrier and is licensed to shipyards in a number of countries. Moss Rosenberg belongs to the Kværner Group, Norway's leading mechanical engineering combine.

Left: General cargo and container ships form only a small part of Norway's merchant fleet in tonnage terms, but more than 60 regular lines are operated by Norwegian shipowners. Innovatory vessel designs have had a big impact on efficiency in this sector of the shipping industry.

Key developments here include the emergence of the roll-on/roll-off concept, door-to-door container transport and ships with new loading and unloading equipment. The container ship *Høegh Musketeer* is pictured here in Antwerp.

Below: Offshore supply ships have a number of subsidiary functions according to design and size – including fire-fighting, emergency evacuation, diving support and anchor-handling.

One of the Norwegian companies which has built up a substantial involvement in the offshore sector is Wilh. Wilhelmsen of Oslo, owner of this fire-fighting unit. In addition to 21 modern liner ships, the Wilhelmsen fleet in operation and on order includes seven rigs and 42 support ships.

New vessel types have made international maritime transport ever faster, cheaper and more effective. Recent innovations include the float-on/float-off concept, pictured below. Such ships can be partly submerged so that the midships section is under water, thus allowing particularly heavy or unwieldy cargoes to be floated onto them. After the ballast water has been pumped out again, the vessel returns to a normal position.

The first two ships of this type were built at Norway's Kaldnes Mek. Verksted shipyard in Tønsberg south of Oslo for one of the most successful Norwegian shipping companies of the past generation, the Oslo-based Jan Erik Dyvi Skipsrederi. This firm was an early specialist in car-carrying, currently operates a number of oil drilling rigs and has moved into a new cargo field with its two latest deliveries.

Dyvi Swan and *Dyvi Tern* can both take deck loads of up to 25 000 tonnes, and are capable of loading or unloading in the space of six hours. During these operations, their midships sections can be submerged to a

depth of seven metres. A speed of 16 knots makes them
significantly faster over long distances than alternative
transport solutions for heavy loads such as barges, and
they are less vulnerable to weather conditions.

Two jack-up drilling rigs owned by Norway's Nordrill
company are seen here being loaded on the *Dyvi Swan* in
Singapore for shipment to Houston.

Sun-starved holiday-makers escaping from northern winters provide the main market for the world's luxury cruise liners. But when Norwegian cruise ships a little more than a century ago initiated an activity that was to grow into today's major industry, the central attraction was Norway's fjords and the passengers came from Britain.

Preceding pages: The Norwegian-owned cruise liner *Royal Viking Sky* glides like a stately swan past Alaska's spectacular glaciers.

Above: The west Norwegian fjords are an attractive destination for domestic and foreign cruise liners alike during the summer. The *Royal Viking Star* is a regular visitor to the Sogne Fjord on sunny June days.

Right: Norway's leading position in Caribbean cruise traffic is aptly illustrated by this scene from the US Virgin Islands, where no less than three of the ships pictured are Norwegian.

Norwegian operators own 13 of the 100 or so vessels that make up the world's cruise fleet. Most of the Norwegian ships operate in the Caribbean with Miami as their base. Since companies from Norway developed cruise traffic from Florida in the late 1960's, liners specially-built for cruising have become more and more luxurious and costly. A ship being introduced by Royal Caribbean Cruise Line at the end of 1982 will carry up to 1500 passengers and cost roughly NOK 700 million.

Largest of all the cruise liners is the 70 000 ton S/S *Norway,* once the French giant on the Atlantic passenger run, *France.* After a thorough conversion, the *Norway* began operating weekly cruises in the Caribbean from 1981. It is pictured above on its one and only visit to Oslo, sailing into the harbour of its home port surrounded by an armada of small boats.

A considerable proportion of the seamen on Norwegian merchant ships are recruited from parts of the country where other employment opportunities are limited. Their earnings are often above the levels paid in mainland Norway and shipping provides both jobs and a source of income for municipalities with a weak economic base.

High standards of quality and reliability are essential if the Norwegian fleet is to maintain its international position. Such requirements have become even more crucial as ships get increasingly complex and competition grows from countries with lower wage levels. The skills and competence of Norwegian seamen are therefore a decisive condition for future success, in the same way that they have been an important factor in the earlier development of Norwegian shipping.

The crew of a modern ship is responsible for a very valuable asset and faces many technical challenges. Maritime training in Norway has been extended to safeguard the recruitment of specialised shipping personnel, and education at the maritime colleges includes engineering courses which – together with practical experience on board – give key crew members the skills to operate and maintain advanced ship's equipment.

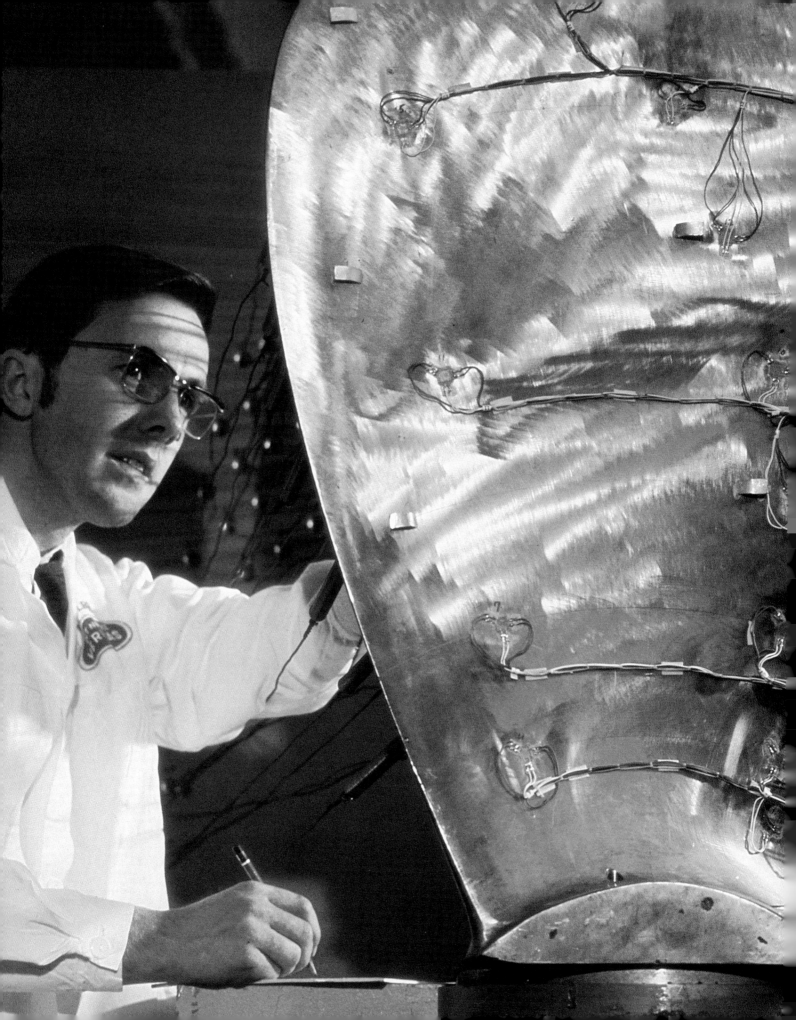

Left: A comprehensive maritime environment has been developed on the basis of Norway's shipping operations, including a number of service activities with great significance for the Norwegian economy.

This close-knit group of fabrication and service functions embraces such elements as education and training facilities, research and development institutions, technical consultant firms, naval architects, shipbroking, insurance, banking, financial services and ship classification.

The latter activity – crucial for structural and operational safety – is handled by Det norske Veritas, which has developed into a world-wide organisation with almost 2 000 employees and 276 offices in 100 countries. Veritas has expanded beyond the shipping sector, too, and the organisation now offers services to a number of other industries.

Above: Norway can boast advanced facilities for testing maritime designs and structures, including ships, oil rigs, production platforms and other installations for the offshore sector. This expertise has been further strengthened with the construction of the world's most sophisticated tank for realistic model tests at the Norwegian Hydrodynamic Laboratories in Trondheim.

Measuring 50 x 80 metres, the tank is exceptionally deep and features a unique moveable bottom that can be adjusted for any depth down to 10 metres. Modern wave-making and current-generating machinery is able to produce a very wide variety of sea states with the aim of subjecting models to the kind of extreme conditions that could be encountered in real life.

A number of other specialised research institutions have also grown up around the Norwegian Institute of Technology in Trondheim, including the SINTEF foundation for scientific and industrial research. With more than 1100 staff, this organisation covers a number of disciplines and makes an important contribution to the development of Norwegian technology. Particular attention is being paid to offshore research.

Shipbuilding is an important industry in a number of Norwegian coastal communities. For generations, the main source of employment in many places has been the construction of vessels for the fishing fleet, coastal traffic or the Norwegian merchant fleet.

A total of 130 shipyards are spread along the Norwegian coast. Of these, a few are large with a thousand or more employees but the great majority are small. One feature common to them all, however, is specialisation in the construction of various ship types.

Above: The Norgas Group has been one of Norway's most expansive and economically successful undertakings in recent times. Its diversified manufacturing and trading activities range from industrial gases and welding equipment to hospital products and pharmaceuticals. International sales account for a steadily growing share of turnover.

One of the group's most successful members is Unitor Ships Service, a supplier of standadised products and services to the international shipping and offshore industries, where the parent Norgas A/S company has a 54 per cent share. Unitor is represented in 450 ports throughout the world. The recent acquisition of Dutch welding specialist Smitweld has also given Norgas a base within the EEC.

94

When it comes to large bulk carriers and oil tankers, Norwegian yards cannot compete with low-cost shipbuilders in the Far East. But Norwaty is well-equipped to take orders on the international market for tonnage specially tailored to meet specific transport needs – indeed, it would be difficult to find a ship type beyond the capability of Norwegian designers and builders.

Many of today's most advanced ship designs have been developed by Norwegian naval architects and these vessels are built not only in Norway but also on licence in many other countries.

Two of the yards found around the shores of the Oslo Fjord are Horten Verft and Kaldnes Mekaniske Verksted, where these pictures were taken.

After several years of unsuccessful exploration for oil in the Norwegian North Sea sector, the Ekofisk field was discovered in 1969 when some of the oil companies with concessions in these waters had already begun to cut back their drilling programmes. It took 10 years and NOK 30 billion to put the Ekofisk find and six other nearby oil and gas discoveries into production. The development includes 22 permanently manned platforms, and the riches hidden 300 metres below the sea surface have called forth innovative technical solutions that advance the frontiers of technology in the offshore industry. The Ekofisk Centre is pictured here.

From adventure to everyday affair

LESS THAN 15 years after the first petroleum find was made on the Norwegian continental shelf, the offshore industry has become an everyday affair – but with great economic significance for the whole community. North Sea oil and gas make their presence felt in every area of Norwegian life, for better or worse.

Production reached nearly 50 million tonnes of oil equivalents in 1981, when it accounted for 15 per cent of Norway's gross domestic product. All the same, falling world oil prices and a temporary stagnation in output over the next few years indicate clearly that the traditional Norwegian industrial sectors will continue to play a decisive part in the country's overall economic growth for years to come.

A number of substantial oil fields have already been discovered in Norwegian waters. Several are in production, while development of others is under way or being planned. One find currently subject to detailed study is an enormous oil and gas field originally discovered in block 31/2: Reserves in this structure – which is thought to cover as much as 700 sq. km. and stretch into three neighbouring blocks – have been tentatively put at 600 – 2000 billion cu.m. of gas, plus some oil.

Development plans face problems here as in other parts of the Norwegian shelf, however. The reserves are spread over a large area and lie in more than 300 metres of water, so that innovatory technical solutions for production will be required – nothing unusual for the North Sea.

Step by step, technological expertise has broken down earlier barriers and produced unconventional answers at an astonishingly rapid pace.

The North Sea petroleum discoveries have created
new industries ashore in Norway. Both the oil refinery at
Mongstad north of Bergen on the west coast and the
petrochemical plants in Bamble south of Oslo were established as a direct result of the finding of the Ekofisk
field.

Construction of the Bamble petrochemical plants was
the largest industrial project ever tackled in mainland
Norway. Owned by Norsk Hydro, Saga Petrokjemi and
Statoil, they comprise an ethylene cracker and plants for
the production of chlorine, vinyl chloride monomer and
three polyolefin varieties.

Previous pages: The Statfjord B production platform is the largest concrete gravity base structure in the world to date. Based on the successful Norwegian Condeep design, it is the first of this type with four support columns, weighs 650 000 tonnes and has a total height of 271 metres. With a base area of 18 000 sq.m., the storage cells clustered around the four columns can hold 250 000 tonnes of crude oil. This view from the construction was taken at its Stavanger building site in 1978.

Left: Installing components in a 120-metre-high support shaft.

Below and right: The world's largest crane barge was brought to Stavanger to assist in assembling the Statfjord B deck structure. Spectators could watch at close hand as the eight-storey living-quarters modules were lifted into position. Each of these units weighed 750 tonnes.

When Siemens A/S and A/S Kongsberg Våpenfabrikk joined forces to develop an advanced supervisory control and data acquisition system based on microprocessor technology and aimed at the offshore market, the idea seemed a wild one.

But this SCADA system is already in use on the Statfjord A production platform in the Norwegian North Sea and has been installed in the main control room (below) on the B platform for the same field. It will also be part of the third production unit on Statfjord, and has been ordered by the Mexican state oil company Pemex.

Advantages of the Kongsberg/Siemens system include its flexibility and capacity, which allow it to control a large number of industrial processes and operations while simultaneously boosting the safety of personnel and equipment. Readily adapted to meet customer specifications, the system also saves space, installation time and costs through extensive use of micro-technology. At its heart are two NORD computers manufactured by the rapidly-expanding Norwegian computer company Norsk Data A/S.

Ranked as the largest oil field so far found in the North Sea, the Statfjord discovery lies 180 km. west of the mouth of the Sogne Fjord. A small part of its reserves are on the UK side of the median line with Norway.

The B platform is the second production unit located on the discovery, and will be followed by a third in 1986. Installed at the southern end of the field, it combines drilling, production and accommodation in a single structure and has a daily production capacity of 150 000 barrels.

More than 300 companies, including 150 Norwegian firms, took part in the construction of this colossus. Main contractor for the steel deck was Moss Rosenberg Verft in Stavanger, while Norwegian Contractors built the concrete section with its storage cells and support columns.

Fabrication of Statfjord B was an enormous assignment with heavy demands on accuracy and coordination. In February 1981, the concrete sub-structure – standing 112 metres above the water – was towed from its con-

struction site near Stavanger to the deep waters of the Yrkje Fjord north of that city. Exactly a month later, the massive steel deck followed and was mated with the support unit a week later.

After a further four months of inshore hook-up and completion work, the whole structure was moved out to the field in a ticklish week-long operation that ranks as the world's largest tow operation to date (below). Peak output from the platform will be reached as early as 1984-85, but production should continue until 2010.

While the Statfjord oil is loaded for shipment onto tankers through special buoys out on the field, associated gas from the discovery will be carried in a major pipeline system to Kårstø on the west coast north of Stavanger – the first time that Norwegian North Sea reserves are brought ashore in Norway by this means. The pipeline is being extended to link with the existing gas line from Ekofisk to Emden in West Germany, and will also carry gas from the Heimdal field and other Norwegian discoveries.

Although offshore oil activities off northern Norway will naturally face problems, weather conditions in these waters are not very different from the North Sea. The whole Norwegian coast is ice-free during winter, for instance.

Oil operations in the North Sea and preparations for exploration and development further north have led to the construction of larger and more powerful rigs and supply vessels. New Norwegian designs include the Aker Group's H-3.2 type and the Bingo concept from the Trosvik Group, which are both semi-submersible units intended to drill in extreme conditions where winds can reach 60 knots and waves top 15 metres in height.

The illustration on these pages show that the North Sea is not always on its best behaviour, and that equipment and crews are put to a hard test on board rigs as well as supply ships. All the same, work seldom has to stop because of weather.

Few economic issues have aroused greater discussion in Norway than exploration drilling off its northern coasts. Controversy has primarily raged around safety aspects of this activity. It is natural in a region so dependent on fishing that the impact of offshore drilling on the fisheries should occupy a broad place in the debate. At the same time, the oil industry will clearly create spin-offs and offer fresh opportunities in a part of the country with a narrow economic base and which needs new industrial activities.

Exploration in the far north has initially been limited to the summer months, but is due to be gradually extended as experience builds up. Even so, the pace planned for these waters means that it will take a generation to drill as many wells there as have already been sunk in the North Sea. Since the northern continental shelf is seven times larger than the latter area, too, uncovering all that might be hidden beneath the seabed could take a very long time.

Above: The commencement of exploration activities in the north during spring 1980 meant the end of a long wait for Harstad, the port selected as main base for oil operations on this part of the Norwegian shelf. When the drilling rig *Treasure Seeker* arrived in the harbour, it provided concrete evidence that the waiting was over – even before the leaves had appeared on the trees.

Above left: While *Treasure Seeker* lay in Harstad, local people were invited on board the Aker H-3 type semi-submersible. No less than 1 300 people came on board in the space of a few hours.

Below left: The companies involved in north Norwegian oil exploration have opened offices in Harstad, but preparations are also well advanced in other parts of the region to meet the busy times ahead – which many hope will be the start of a new economic era there. Hammerfest, the world's most northerly town, has been chosen as the advance base to support drilling operations outside Finnmark county.

Just before midnight on a sun-filled June night in 1980, a rock bit from the Wilhelmsen-owned rig *Treasure Seeker* began to drill its way down into the seabed on the Tromsøflaket off Finnmark county. From a drilling point of view the operation was in no way remarkable, but it represented an historic occasion as the start of the oil age in the north. *Ross Rig* joined the hunt a week later.

Encouraging results were achieved from the very first, and the signs are that the data acquired through geological and seismic surveys were right in indicating good prospects for commercial petroleum discoveries in these waters.

All the same, there is a long way to go before possible production can begin – not before 1990 at the earliest. Among the many questions that need to be answered are the types of production installation best suited to the water depths.

Below: Drilling personnel on the semi-submersible *Ross Rig* examine material brought to the surface by the drill bit from beneath the seabed in the far north.

Since the Geophysical Company of Norway – Geco – was founded in 1972, it has developed into one of the world's leading geophysical survey specialists. Understandably enough, the oil companies put a lot of emphasis on obtaining the best possible data about geological formations beneath the seabed before they start drilling. Sinking a well in the North Sea costs NOK 70-80 million, which makes the price of a three-dimensional seismic survey look insignificant by comparison.

Geco is one of the most successful Norwegian companies of recent years and has concentrated on building up a fleet of specialised vessels for seismic work. Most of the 13 ships owned by Geco in 1982 come from yards in the Sunnmøre district of western Norway, and are equipped with the latest technological solutions. Features of these vessels include low noise and vibration levels – important for the kind of surveys they are undertake.

Seismic surveying at sea involves «shooting» air guns towed behind the vessels. The release of compressed air sends impulses through the water and the rocks beneath the seabed, which rebound from different geological formations in a characteristic way that can be recorded on the survey ship and used to build up a picture of rock strata several thousand metres down.

Left top and bottom: The *Geco Delta* at work with the air gun array strung out behind it. A buoy carrying a radar reflector and flashing light is attached to the end of the cable.

Above: Data collected by the Geco ships are analysed at the company's processing centres, including the one in Stavanger.

Europe's first ground station for two-way communication between ship and shore via satellite has been opened at Eik near Stavanger in south-west Norway. The fully-automatic facility will handle traffic to and from vessels in the Indian Ocean and forms part of the international Inmarsat system for maritime satellite communication.

Norwegian telecommunications specialist A.S. Elektrisk Bureau was the main contractor for the advanced equipment installed at the Eik station, and celebrated its 100th anniversary at the time the latter was officially opened. During a century of activity, EB has built up substantial expertise in its field. The company's achievements include the introduction of the first European-made ship-based satellite communications terminal in the mid-1970's. Plans exist to extend EB production to a number of countries.

Sea and air unite the land

Above: Assembly of communication equipment at one of Elektrisk Bureau's nine production plants in Norway.

Right: High mountains riven by narrow inhabited valleys create difficult reception conditions for radio and television in many parts of Norway. Around 200 transmitters have been built to overcome such problems, however. Most of these installations are located on mountain summits and are difficult to reach. Even though the equipment is fully automated, it can be a tough job to keep the transmission links in operation throughout the year under the battering of wind and weather.

Fitters are exposed to full force of the elements as they replace antenna equipment on the 40-metre-high Hestmannen transmitter mast off the coast of Helgeland in northern Norway.

T HE COAST has always been Norway's main highway. Although the country today possesses a well-developed air transport network that links it together through 40 airports, the coastal shipping routes have retained their vital place in the Norwegian communications system.

With its regular daily sailings, the coastal express service provides the backbone of this seaborne traffic. Every single night throughout the year – come rain, fog and storm – one of the ships that serve the «hurtigrute» sets off from Bergen on the 10-day round trip to the little mining town of Kirkenes on the border with the Soviet Union and back.

At the moment, a major newbuilding programme is under way to replace the existing ships with new vessels capable of carrying more than 400 passengers. Due to come into service over the next few years, the latter will continue to provide the core of the coastal transport system. They can also be expected to maintain a reputation as one of the country's biggest tourist attractions.

In its day, the «hurtigrute» service represented a revolution for the people living along the north Norwegian coast. Aircraft produced a fresh transformation, and even small communities in Norway are linked by regular daily flights with the rest of country today.

It is easy to imagine what these air routes mean in a nation with such difficult communication conditions, where long distances, widely scattered settlements, deep fjords cutting into the landscape and high mountains raise all kinds of barriers for land transport. Since an all-year airport was opened at Longyearbyen, the remote Svalbard islands in the far north have also been connected to the international air network.

Because the sea has been the natural routeway in Norway right up to our own times, nearly all the towns grew up along the lengthy coast. With a few exceptions, due mainly to the presence of mineral resources in the mountains or availability of hydro-electric power, most Norwegian urban centres remain by the sea today.

While even the towns out at the mouths of the fjords or on the offshore islands have generally gained road connections with the rest of the country now, ship and ferry links retain their importance. Norway has more than 260 ferry routes along its convoluted coast, and the first Norwegian written legal code – Magnus Lagabøters law of 1274 – sets out the rights and obligations of citizens in connection with ferrying.

Above: The lighthouse service plays an important role in the coastal community because of the many difficult stretches of sea, narrow sounds and rocks as well as the frequent winter storms. But in the summer, northern Norway's lighthouses go out of business for several months as night and day merge into one under the Midnight Sun.

Right: Ålesund in Sunnmøre on the west coast has become the centre for a flourishing and diversified industrial district, which includes the biggest concentration of furniture manufacturers in Norway.

Bridges for road and rail are a common feature of the Norwegian landscape. Every single year, the road network is extended by the addition of several hundred new bridges and there are said to be about 3 000 railway bridges in the country. All the same, a number of island communities along the coast will never be connected to the mainland and cars or passengers must continue to rely on ferry services for crossing many of the fjords that divide the land.

Above: Railway construction in Norway has been a difficult feat of engineering, as shown by the country's many railway bridges such as Kylling Bru in Romsdalen.

Above right: Norway's easternmost town is Vadsø, which faces out towards the Arctic Ocean on an island that will soon be joined to the mainland through the first Norwegian submarine highway tunnel. The 2 800 metre tunnel fulfils an old dream for the 4 000 people who live in the little community on the edge of the Barents Sea.

Below right: One of the largest Norwegian bridge-building projects in recent years has sought to link all the main islands in the Vesterålen group north of the Lofotens by road across such structures as the 1 020-metre Hadsel Bridge.

Roadbuilding is no simple business in Norway, either. The standard of Norwegian highways lies below the levels achieved in many other countries, with few motorways and numerous steep and narrow stretches. But Norwegians have been compelled to accustom themselves to such conditions. With practised skill and stamina, plus a bit of patience, they generally manage to gain the upper hand over nature's whims – even when winter storms and snow try to put additional spokes in their wheels.

The trains run more or less normally all through the year and the airports are kept open with the aid of snow-ploughs, fog dispersants and de-icing. Motorists are not so lucky. Snow gets cleared from the city streets without too many problems, but in the mountains long-distance travellers can be faced with the choice of waiting until the passes have been cleared or loading their cars onto railway trucks.

Despite the construction of tunnels through the mountains, many roads in the highland areas are closed throughout the winter, and spring is well advanced before it becomes possible to drive across the Hardangervidda plateau between Oslo and Bergen.

Above: Both reindeer and elk can be encountered on Norwegian roads, like these reindeer crossing the highway far to the north in Finnmark.

Right: Motorways are not a common sight in Norway, but here the E18 winds through the city of Drammen near Oslo.

120

The whole population turns out to participate in the festivities on Norway's two national days, May 17 and the Holmenkollen Day in March. These are the occasions when the broadest cross-section of the Norwegian people can be seen assembled together.

May 17 is Constitution Day, when spring arrives. In contrast, Holmenkollen Day always falls on a Sunday, when a teeming multitude makes its way from Oslo up to the world-famed Holmenkollen ski jump that stands as a white landmark on the hills overlooking the city. The occasion is a national sporting event and popular festival, with hundreds of thousands of spectators gathered round the jump to watch the world's greatest exponents of this daring and spectacular sport.

In tune with Nature

Shipbuilding draws on generations of skill.

Work at sea encourages good appetites.

Even the youngest enjoy the music of May 17.

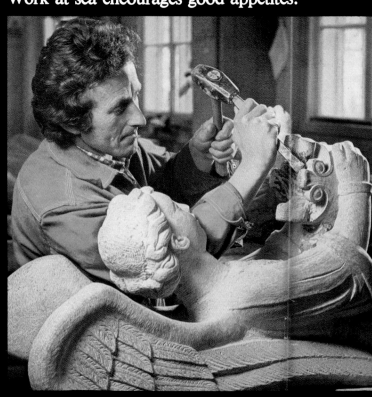

Restoring a national historic monument.

West coast spring under snow-clad mountains

Between sea and sky...

Off to wrest oil wealth from the sea.

Winter is the season for children – the time of wet snowflakes on young faces, cold winter sunshine over snow-covered landscapes, skiing schools, ski trips in forest and mountains and fishing on the ice. Hundreds of holes cut or drilled in the ice over fjords or small lakes provide convincing evidence of the popularity of ice fishing among adults and children alike.

Left: Winter is playtime in the snow.

Far right: Where's that fish?

Centre: Only 100 people live at Skjånes on the Nordkyn peninsula in Finnmark county far to the north. This little fishing community has its own school, where children from the surrounding district have to board.

But there are no roads to Skjånes and the only winter link is by snow scooter across country to the town of Mehamn 40 km. away. Another alternative is a local passenger boat service that takes a long time and only runs three times a week. So doctor, priest and youngsters on their way to a dance stick to the snow scooter.

126

HM King Olav V has followed the whole of modern Norway's growth and development as an independent nation from the inside. He took part in his first Council of State with Cabinet Ministers as early as 1921, and has participated in most of these weekly meetings during the subsequent 60 years. In 1982, he reached the 25th anniversary of his accession to the Norwegian throne and will celebrate his 80th birthday the following year.

As the monarch of a small country, King Olav is an inseparable member of the Norwegian family. His charm and abilities have won him friends and respect at all levels in the community, and as head of state he is in the unusual position of enjoying support for the monarchy from representatives of all parties, both to the right and left.

The King has secured and maintained contact with people throughout the country by his presence at events and arrangements large and small, and it would be impossible to count the number of ceremonies and – not least – sporting occasions he has graced with his attendance.

An active sportsman despite his age, King Olav remains a keen skier and there are no signs that he has taken the tiller in his last yachting contest. As a sailor, he has represented Norway in the Olympic Games and world championships and remains as feared a competitor as ever.

The personal warmth and smiling humanity that help to make the King so popular among his people are captured in this picture outside the Gol stave church in Oslo's Folk Museum, one of the 31 examples of a unique style of church architecture preserved in Norway. The stave churches and the Viking ships represent the creative peak of mediaeval Norwegian skill at building and carving in wood.

128

With only three per cent of Norway's territory and 300 000 inhabitants, it might sound like delusions of grandeur to claim that Rogaland county would have coped admirably as an independent country. This region on the south-west coast is Norway in miniature, however. Not only has it become the centre of the Norwegian oil industry, with a number of significant fabrication companies involved in offshore-related work, but it also ranks as a highly important agricultural district with the country's most diversified and intensive farm activities.

Here are to be found Europe's biggest plough factory, the largest bicycle manufacturer in the Nordic region, Norway's most important plant for prefabricated houses and the centre for the Norwegian fish canning industry. Important textile firms and suppliers of fishing industry equipment have their bases in Rogaland, while manufactures of technically-sophisticated robots or quality furniture provide other examples of the variety of expansive industries to be found there.

Production of ploughs *(right)*, industrial robots *(below)* and bicycles *(far right)* are some of the characteristic manufacturing activities in Norway's oil county.

Norway is the European country with the shortest opera tradition, but can claim on the other hand long experience in the export of opera singers – to be found working today in many parts of the world. One of the great interpreters of Strauss and Wagner in our time is the dramatic soprano Ingrid Bjoner, who has starred at most of Europe's greatest opera houses. She is pictured here in the title role from Puccini's *Turandot* in Budapest.

New vitality from old tradition

THE FIRST evidence for some form of artistic activity in Norway is the lively pictures of elk, reindeer and deer carved into rock faces between 4000 and 9000 years ago. Later came rock carvings of people and ships, followed by intricate animal ornamentation.

An independent Norwegian art has only emerged at certain periods in the country's history. One example of such native creativity is the imaginative wood-carving artistry that can be seen on Viking ships or stave churches.

Three Viking vessels have been excavated in Norway, providing an unusual insight into the lifestyle, farming methods and handicraft developments of these early Norwegians. Their ships were built to sail the open seas, and the 22-metre Oseberg ship is the finest example of the outstanding craft skills of the Viking Age. It also provides visible evidence of the traditions that underlie Norwegian shipbuilding industry.

Wood-carving artistry developed still further in the stave churches, an architectronic form without parallel elsewhere that flourished in Norway from the 12th century AD.

Long winters encouraged men and women in the isolated rural communities to cultivate and develop a variety of handicrafts and decorative forms. As a result, characteristic traditions and styles have existed right up to our own times in fields such as weaving and furniture-making. Today's Norwegian tapestry weavers and the output of around 200 furniture factories nourish these traditions – and make them available outside Norway, too.

Few Norwegians have succeeded in influencing cultural life on an international scale. Some giants nevertheless made a great impact on the wider world of art. Among pictorial artists, the most significant is Edvard Munch.

Gustav Vigeland was the first great Norwegian sculptor of modern times. His masterpiece is the great collection of sculptures laid out to form a unified whole in Oslo's Frogner Park.

The unquestioned master among Norwegian dramatists is Henrik Ibsen, whose plays are staged in many languages and remain as relevant today as when they were written during the 19th century. Ibsen's unique understanding of the female temperament, in particular, makes his women immortal.

In the field of music, the name most strongly associated with Norway is Edvard Grieg. The old Norwegian folk melodies live on through his work, which carried them out into the wide world. Grieg's *Concerto in A Minor* is among the most popular works of orchestral music.

Some representatives of today's artistic life in Norway are presented on the following pages. They include artists with deep roots in old Norwegian cultural traditions and others who are strongly influenced by European trends.

The first Norwegian composer since Edvard Grieg to achieve real international recognition is Arne Nordheim. While Grieg's music was rooted in national tradition, the latter derives his tonal language from Europe and receives commissions from all over the world. Nordheim was a pioneer of electronic music, but today the large living orchestra is his main instrument of expression. Among his best known works are a number of ballets, and many choreographers have ordered new music from Nordheim for their works. The composer's latest success in this field is the full-length ballet *The Tempest,* based on the Shakespearean play. This work has played all over Europe and in the USA, and is danced here by Ketil Gudim at the Norwegian Opera in Oslo.

Actress Liv Ullmann is unquestionably the most famous Norwegian artiste of our time, and has appeared in American films and on Broadway as well as in Europe. She gained particular fame from her collaboration with the Swedish film director Ingmar Bergman, but has also become well-known in recent years for her substantial contribution to humanitarian activities. As a good-will ambassador for UNESCO, she has contributed to exposing unacceptable conditions in disaster areas – particularly for children.

Her latest screen project is a film version of the novel *Jenny* by Norway's Nobel Literature Prize winner Sigrid Undset. Made as a Norwegian/West German/Italian co-production for television, the film includes scenes from Rome and Oslo.

Norway has emerged as a centre for jazz over the past two decades, with two major annual festivals devoted to this music, in Kongsberg and Molde.

Both older established musicians and young newcomers flock to these occasions and the jazz environment around them – together with a faithful and committed international audience.

Probably as a result of the festivals, a number of lead-ing Norwegian jazz musicians are active today. Saxophonist Jan Garbarek belongs in the front rank of this group, and has built up an international reputation through his personal playing style and more than 30 LPs. Another internationally acclaimed jazz name is Karin Krogh. She and Garbarek have topped the popularity polls of American jazz magazines.

Edvard Munch's vast output of paintings and graphic art from the end of the last century to his death in 1943 is a timeless statement on human fates created from his own heart's blood. During the last decades of his life, Munch never sold a painting, as he considered them to be his «children». On his death, the enormous collection he had built up was left to the city of Oslo, which built a special museum to display it.

Left: Frans Widerberg and Svein Strand are two of the most prominent of Norway's younger painters today. Characteristic for Widerberg is his use of primary colours in works crackling with fiery reds and yellows or shining with clear green and blue. Their subjects are mankind's life, the difficulties of living, the human struggle against suffering, with nature and themselves, loneliness and relations with the surrounding world.

This page: Svein Strand is the most un-Norwegian of the country's contemporary painters. He has lived in the Mediterranean area for 10 years and draws his inspiration from France. His canvases do not depict nature, but interiors and still-lifes. He often introduces mirrors or doors opening into other rooms and the paintings abound with ornamental detail. With his subdued, slightly blurred pigments, Strand emerges as a subtle colourist.

Silversmith Toril Bjorg and artist in glass Ulla Mari Brantberg have collaborated fruitfully for several years at the Frysja craft centre in Oslo. Their silver spoons with glass handles attract considerable attention at exhibitions.

The first materials used by Toril Bjorg were fragments of broken glass that she collected along the seashore and framed in silver. Today, she and Ulla Mari Brantberg represent new and young trends in Norwegian handicrafts.

Toril Bjorg argues that she creates «silver jewellery for jeans», and regards her pieces as a continuation of Norway's old rural silverwork traditions. The country silversmiths whose roots lie in Norwegian folk art are still alive and have founded a number of small companies that also export silverware.

The finest traditions of Norwegian tapestry weaving are continued in the work of Synnøve Anker Aurdal. Her tapestries are inspired by old weaving techniques, but she remains just as much a pioneer in contemporary art. In her quiet way, she has carried tapestry work over from the figurative to pure abstract forms and been accepted by critics and public alike. Her many well-known wall-hangings include the ones adorning the 800-year-old Håkonshallen hall in Bergen and the Iceland Tapestry – Norway's national gift to the Icelanders on their 1000th anniversary. Synnøve Aurdal is the Norwegian representative at the Venice Biennial in 1982.

Below: Arnold Haukeland heralded a break with the naturalist style that dominated post-1945 Norwegian sculpture. His power and vitality, expressed in non-figurative forms that reach avidly for the stars, are in accord with the untamed elements in Norwegian nature and spirit. His many works include a «sound-sculpture» for the blind, fashioned in collaboration with the composer Arne Nordheim. The sculpture seen here is located outside the head office of the Norwegian insurance company, Storebrand, in Oslo.

Right: Sculptor Knut Steen has changed his style radically since he completed the Whaling Monument during the 1960's. But the Monument, which swings through 360 degrees on its axis in the course of a day, remains a landmark in the prosperous industrial and holiday port of Sandefjord in south-east Norway that was once one of the world's great whaling centres.

Today, Steen creates subtle, slender sculptures, depicting Man and Woman in musical lines. Two of his latest works adorn the recently-built Oslo Concert House.

© by The Export Council of Norway
and Grøndahl & Søn A.s.
Oslo 1982

Photo-composition,
reproduction, and printing
by Aske Trykkeri A.s, Stavanger

Binding by Kristoffer Johnsen, Skien

ISBN 82-504-0557-9

PHOTOGRAPHERS:

Front cover: Vidar Opsahl
Back cover: Johan Brun
Inside cover: Kjell Witberg

page 1:   Rolf M. Aagaard
page 2:   Rolf M. Aagaaard
page 3:   Terje S. Knudsen (2)
                 (bottom) Vidar Opsahl
page 4-5:   Johan Brun
page 6-7:   To-Foto
page 8:   Terje Gustavsen
page 9:   Rolf M. Aagaard
page 10:   Trygve Skramstad
page 11:   Kim Hart
page 12:   A-foto
page 13:   Fjellanger-Widerøe
page 14:   Kim Hart
page 15:   Husmo-Foto
page 16:   Eivind Fossheim
page 17:   Husmo-Foto
page 18:   Sverre Bergli
page 19:   Husmo-Foto
page 20:   Knudsens Fotocenter
page 21:   Jon Hauge
page 22-23:   Fjellanger-Widerøe
page 24:   Marvin Newman
page 25:   Terje S. Knudsen
page 26:   (left) Arne Svendsen
page 26:   (right) Rude Foto
page 27:   Per O. Breifjell
page 28:   Per O. Breifjell
page 29:   Sigbjørn Henanger
page 30-31:   Julian Charrington
page 32:   (bottom) Terje S. Knudsen
page 33-35:   Terje S. Knudsen
page 36:   Julian Charrington
page 37:   Rolf Riise
page 38-39:   S.A. Nordby

page 40-41:   Johan Brun
page 43-50:   Sverre M. Fjelstad
page 51:   (bottom right) Sverre M. Fjelstad
page 51:   (above and bottom left) To-Foto
page 52:   Svein Oppegaard
page 53:   Rolf Bjørnstad
page 54-55:   Oskar Torrissen
page 57:   (above) Geir Arnesen
page 57:   (bottom) Oskar Torrissen
page 58:   Husmo-Foto
page 59:   Tom A. Kalstad
page 60-61:   To-Foto
page 62-63:   (above) To-Foto
page 62-63:   (bottom) Husmo-Foto
page 63:   (bottom right) Rolf M. Aagaard
page 64-65:   To-Foto
page 68:   Kim Hart
page 69:   Per Gran
page 70:   Terje Gustavsen
page 71:   Kim Hart
page 72:   Johan Brun
page 74:   Eivind Fossheim
page 75:   Rolf M. Aagaard
page 76:   A-foto
page 77:   Kim Hart
page 78-82:   Knut Vadseth
page 83:   Torbjørn Lien
page 84-85:   Frederick R.Y. Tan
page 88:   Knut Snare
page 88-89:   (above) A-foto
page 88-89:   (bottom) Per H. Houge
page 90-91:   Knut Vadseth
page 93:   Bjørn Johansen
page 94:   Tore Kopperud
page 94-95:   Ragge Strand
page 98-99:   Jan M. Pedersen
page 100-101:   Vidar Opsahl
page 102-103:   (above) Agne Rømmingen
page 104-105:   Vidar Opsahl
page 107:   Tormod Wanvik

page 108:   (bottom) Terje S. Knudsen
page 108:   (above) Kåre Foss
page 109:   Kåre Foss
page 110:   Leif Berge
page 111:   Leif Berge
page 112-113:   Jim Bengtson
page 115:   Magnar Kirknes
page 116:   Øystein Kristiansen
page 117:   Husmo-Foto
page 118:   Husmo-Foto
page 119:   (above) Jostein Drevdal
page 119:   (bottom) Vidar Opsahl
page 120:   Terje Gustavsen
page 121:   Øystein Kristiansen
page 122-123:   Kim Hart
page 124:   (top left) Ragge Strand
page 124:   (bottom left) Johan Brun
page 124:   (top right) Knut Vadseth
page 125:   (top) A-foto
page 125:   (bottom left) Kim Hart
page 125:   (bottom right) Terje S. Knudsen
page 126:   Johan Brun
page 126-127:   Rolf M. Aagaard
page 127:   Husmo-Foto
page 128-129:   Dag Grundseth
page 130-131:   Rolf M. Aagaard
page 132-133:   Janos Czak
page 135:   Karsten Bundgaard
page 136:   (above left and right) Sverre Bergli
page 136:   (bottom left) Svein Erik Furulund
page 137:   NTB
page 138:   Rolf M. Aagaard
page 139:   (above) O. Væring
page 139:   (bottom) Aage Owe
page 140-141:   Rolf M. Aagaard
page 142:   Kim Hart
page 143:   Kim Hart

*It has unfortunately proved impossible to ascertain the
name of the photographer for some of the photos in this
publication.*